P9-DMR-081

Little Lions, Bull Baiters & Hunting Hounds

A HISTORY OF DOG BREEDS

WRITTEN AND ILLUSTRATED BY

JEFF CROSBY AND SHELLEY ANN JACKSON

Tundra Books

For our families, both human and canine.
– JC & SJ

This book was generously supported by
the Society of Children's Book Writers and Illustrators.

A portion of the proceeds from this book will be donated to
animal welfare and rescue organizations.

Published in Canada by Tundra Books,
75 Sherbourne Street, Toronto, Ontario M5A 2P9

Published in the United States by Tundra Books of Northern New York,
P.O. Box 1030, Plattsburgh, New York 12901

Library of Congress Control Number: 2007927387

Library and Archives Canada Cataloguing in Publication

Little lions, bull baiters & hunting hounds : a history of dog breeds /
Jeff Crosby and Shelley Ann Jackson, authors and illustrators.

Includes bibliographical references.
ISBN 978-0-88776-815-6

1. Dog breeds – Juvenile literature. 2. Dogs – Juvenile literature. I. Jackson, Shelley Ann
II. Title. III. Title: Little lions, bull baiters & hunting hounds.

SF426.5.C76 2008 j636.7'1 C2007-902723-7

We acknowledge the financial support of the Government of Canada through the
Book Publishing Industry Development Program (BPIDP) and that of the Government of Ontario
through the Ontario Media Development Corporation's Ontario Book Initiative.

We further acknowledge the support of the Canada Council for the Arts
and the Ontario Arts Council for our publishing program.

Design: Jeff Crosby and Shelley Ann Jackson

Printed and bound in Singapore

1 2 3 4 5 6 13 12 11 10 09 08

Contents

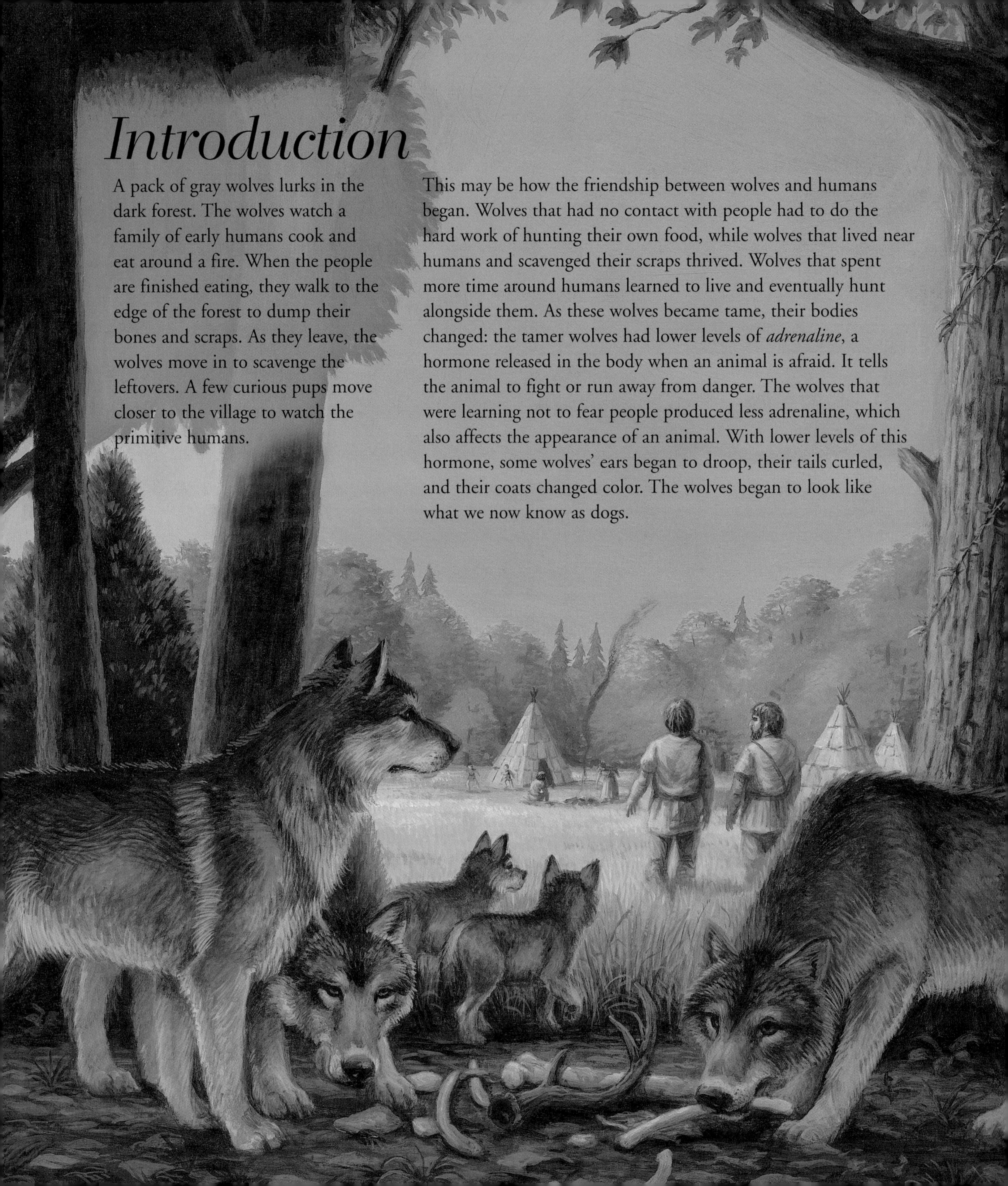

Introduction

A pack of gray wolves lurks in the dark forest. The wolves watch a family of early humans cook and eat around a fire. When the people are finished eating, they walk to the edge of the forest to dump their bones and scraps. As they leave, the wolves move in to scavenge the leftovers. A few curious pups move closer to the village to watch the primitive humans.

This may be how the friendship between wolves and humans began. Wolves that had no contact with people had to do the hard work of hunting their own food, while wolves that lived near humans and scavenged their scraps thrived. Wolves that spent more time around humans learned to live and eventually hunt alongside them. As these wolves became tame, their bodies changed: the tamer wolves had lower levels of *adrenaline*, a hormone released in the body when an animal is afraid. It tells the animal to fight or run away from danger. The wolves that were learning not to fear people produced less adrenaline, which also affects the appearance of an animal. With lower levels of this hormone, some wolves' ears began to droop, their tails curled, and their coats changed color. The wolves began to look like what we now know as dogs.

A pack of dogs tears through the tall grass, chasing a quick hare. One long-legged dog is faster than the others. It snatches up the hare and shakes it. The dog proudly trots back to the human hunter with its catch, while the others follow. This dog will be rewarded with food and will grow to be stronger and healthier than the slower dogs. It will mate and produce puppies that will also become long-legged fast hunters.

When humans migrated to different areas around the world thousands of years ago, they took dogs with them. To survive, the dogs had to adapt to new surroundings. One example of adaptation is superb eyesight. Only dogs with the best eyesight would have been able to spot prey off in the distance. These dogs were nurtured and bred. With each generation, the dogs' eyesight became sharper until eventually, it was much better than that of wolves. Another adaptation is webbed feet. All dogs have some skin connecting their toes, but the more skin a dog has, the stronger and faster it can swim. So, the best swimmers were bred and, as a result, today's water dogs have webbed feet.

In time, humans realized that they could mate certain dogs to bring out the features they liked. They began to create breeds with special skills – short-legged dogs to hunt in small spaces, hardy dogs to withstand extreme climates, and fierce dogs for fighting. Royals were the first to breed dogs that didn't do any work – only the highborn could afford such a luxury. They often bred lapdogs to be small and cute. The general public began to keep dogs as pets in the 1800s, when breed-specific clubs were formed, and dog shows became a popular entertainment.

Today there are over four hundred different breeds of dogs. A breed is a group of dogs with common ancestors that have similar characteristics. Each has been shaped by its geographic home and the job it was bred to do. Upon examination, you can see how a breed's history has influenced the way the dog appears and behaves today. Because there are so many breeds, they are not all in this book. The breeds represented here were selected to show as much variety in geography, appearance, and function as possible. They are grouped into four main categories, according to their original purpose. The four categories: hunting, herding, working, and companion are presented in the order that they were most likely developed.

Hunting Breeds

Hunting is probably the first job that dogs did for man, and *sighthounds* are possibly the oldest type of hunting dog. Sighthounds spot prey with their superb eyesight. Their long legs give them the height to see over great distances and the speed needed to chase their prey down. Sighthounds have narrow heads and lean bodies for speed. They hunt silently, like wolves.

THE GREYHOUND, A SIGHTHOUND.

THE BLOODHOUND, A SCENTHOUND.

Scenthounds are a different type of hunter. They use their well-developed sense of smell to track prey. They mainly follow the scent trail left by an animal on the ground. They are slower and heavier than sighthounds. Like wolves, scenthounds hunt in packs, but they bark loudly when scenting, to let the hunter know where to follow.

Sporting breeds are hunters bred specifically to locate birds. They don't catch the birds, but they find them for the hunter, flush them out of bushes, or even retrieve birds after they have been shot. Setters, spaniels, pointers, and retrievers are all sporting breeds with unique working styles. Unlike scenthounds that search for scent left by mammals on the ground, sporting breeds search for scent left by birds in the air.

The Vizsla, a sporting breed.

Terriers are yet another type of hunting dog. The word *terrier* comes from the Latin word *terra*, which means "earth." Terriers got this name because they chased prey from their burrows or dug the pests out of the earth. Terriers are usually small and quick like their prey, and are expert diggers. They often work on their own, without direction from a human hunter.

The Cairn, a terrier.

Afghan Hound

The Afghan Hound was developed from sighthounds, brought to Afghanistan by Persian settlers in the 6th century. It was trained by nomadic Afghan tribes to hunt speedy prey such as hare and gazelle. The hounds were much faster than the hunters who followed them on horseback, so they had to think on their own. They are well built for mountainous Afghanistan. Afghan Hounds have wide hips that help them run over rough, rocky terrain and large feet that allow them to make quick turns. They are very fast and can leap great distances. Except on the face and along the spine, the coat is thick and long, protecting it during the cold winter. True to its history of spotting far-off prey, the Afghan Hound is one of the few dogs that notices birds and planes flying through the sky.

Guidance from above? Often when the Afghan Hound hunted, it watched for direction from a trained hawk flying overhead. The Hound could tell by the hawk's movement that it had found prey. The hawk swooped at the prey to chase it toward the dog.

Near the end of the Middle Ages, Russian aristocrats began breeding sighthounds, which they designed to look noble and beautiful. They focused on bringing out certain physical traits, such as silky coats and long graceful legs. The resulting *Borzoi* (pronounced BOR-zoy), which means "swift" in Russian, was used for grand ceremonial wolf hunts. In Imperial Russia, only the wealthy could afford to hunt and eat meat. The nobility were so well off, they could even spend time hunting animals that they didn't eat, such as the wolf. Often hundreds of Borzois, scenthounds, aristocrats, and serfs took part in wolf hunts. After the scenthounds located a wolf, a pair of Borzois was sent after it. They worked together to knock the wolf down and then hold it for the hunter. The wolf was often later released. Indoors, the Borzoi is calm and well mannered, but outside, it is remarkably quick and will chase anything that moves.

Borzoi

Downfall of a dog. The Borzoi became a symbol of the Russian nobility's imperial power. During the 1917 Russian Revolution, the nobility was overthrown and most Borzois in Russia were killed. Luckily, the czar had given many dogs as gifts to visiting royalty. It is through these dogs that the breed continued.

Greyhound

The Greyhound is the fastest sprinter of all dogs. Its narrow head and body cut through the wind, while its long, graceful legs glide over the ground with lightening speed. Its large lungs hold lots of air to power it while it runs. In ancient times, this sighthound was used in the Middle East for hunting, and later it spread throughout Europe. The English took advantage of its speed and hunting skills to develop a sport called hare coursing (a race during which several dogs chase a hare over a marked area). This popular entertainment evolved into dog racing in

the United States when a mechanical rabbit was invented in 1912. Today, the Greyhound is best known as a racing dog. It can run up to forty-five miles per hour – almost as fast as a racehorse. Sadly, after a Greyhound's racing career ends, it is often killed. Thousands more lose their lives each year because the racing industry breeds a huge quantity of dogs and then selects only the fastest for racing. There are clubs that rescue and find homes for as many of these animals as possible. Once the Greyhound is trained not to chase other pets, it makes a gentle and loving family dog. Its ability to relax and blend in with the family has earned it the nickname, "World's Fastest Couch Potato."

Can a dog be too good at hunting? Often in Medieval times, the king was the only one allowed to hunt in the forest. Greyhounds were such skilled hunters that if a common person's hound was found near the forest, the owner had to pay a fine. If it was caught *in* the forest, it became the property of the king.

Irish Wolfhound

The Irish Wolfhound was a hunter and war dog for the Celts over two thousand years ago. These gray sighthounds were courageous enough to hunt wolves and massive red deer. They had to be enormous and strong to pull men off of their horses or out of chariots during battle. By the 1700s, few people were raising Wolfhounds because the wolf and elk had been hunted to extinction in Ireland. Also, many of the dogs had been given as gifts to visiting royalty. The number of Irish Wolfhounds became so low that a British army captain was concerned they would soon be extinct. In 1869 he found the few Wolfhounds that remained in the country and bred them to other similar dogs, saving the breed. Today's Irish Wolfhound is the tallest dog breed, measuring up to 3 feet (91 cm) at the shoulders. Wolfhounds need a lot of space in a home – their long, powerful tails can knock things over when simply wagging back and forth.

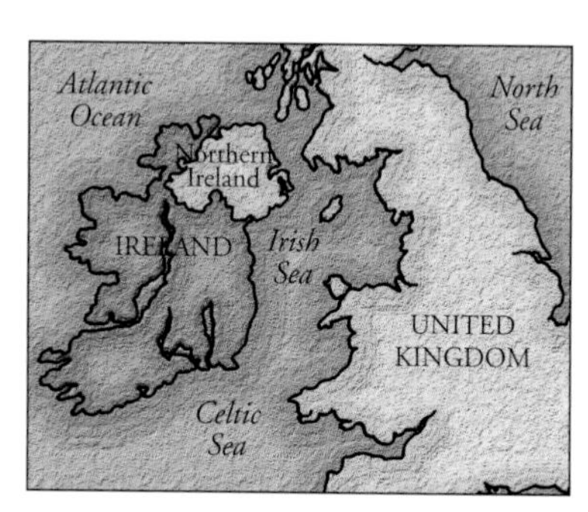

Can a vicious beast be tamed?
Irish Wolfhounds were so ferocious, they commonly killed the animals they hunted and the men they attacked. But they have been bred as pets for many years and are now calm and sweet. Irish Wolfhounds are sometimes called Gentle Giants.

Rhodesian Ridgeback

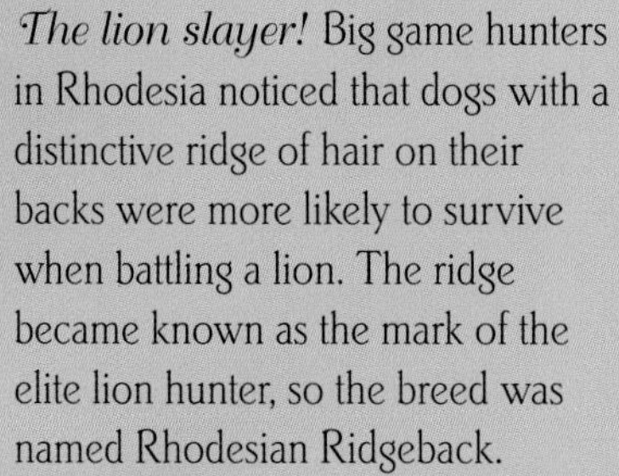

The lion slayer! Big game hunters in Rhodesia noticed that dogs with a distinctive ridge of hair on their backs were more likely to survive when battling a lion. The ridge became known as the mark of the elite lion hunter, so the breed was named Rhodesian Ridgeback.

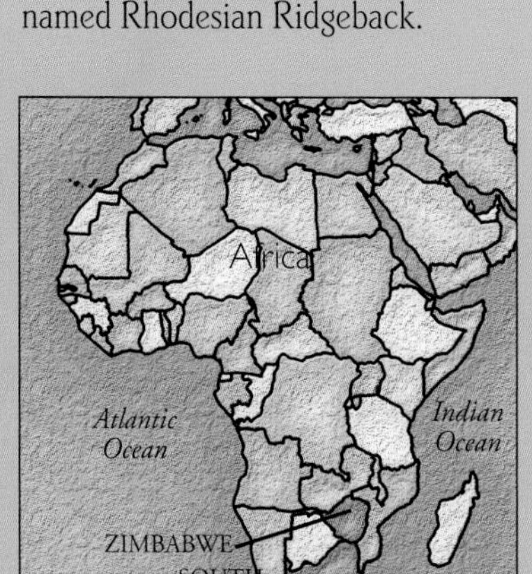

In South Africa in the 16th and 17th centuries, there was a breed of sighthound kept by the native Hottentot tribe. This breed had a ridge of hair growing backwards along the spine. When Dutch settlers arrived, they bred their European hunting dogs with the Hottentot dog. They created an amazing new breed that could withstand the extreme heat of the South African days and the freezing night temperatures. It could handle the thick, thorny African bush and go a day or more without water. It not only hunted, but also guarded the farm and protected its owner when he was camping alone in the bush. In 1870, several of these dogs were introduced to Rhodesia (now Zimbabwe), where they became famous as skilled lion hunters. True to their history as silent trackers, Rhodesian Ridgebacks only bark when there is something important they want their owner to see.

Bloodhound

The Bloodhound is thought to be the oldest scenthound. It is large and slow with long drooping ears and an unrivaled nose. Originally, Bloodhounds were used for hunting deer. In 1066, William the Conqueror introduced them to England. Within one hundred years, most English monasteries kept packs of Bloodhounds for hunting. They were selectively bred so that they were always of pure blood, earning them their name. Eventually, the Bloodhound became famous for its ability to track criminals and lost people. After smelling an item that holds a person's scent, it finds and follows the scent trail. Bloodhounds have successfully trailed scents as old as two weeks and as far as 138 miles (222 km). When the Bloodhound locates the person it is tracking, it bays with long, low howls to let everyone know. The gentle Bloodhound will never harm a person that it locates. It may, however, slobber on them, as it is very friendly and prone to drooling.

The nose knows! When a Bloodhound identifies a criminal, it can be used as evidence against him in a court of law. One famous Bloodhound, Nick Carter, was credited with sending over six hundred criminals to prison in the early 1900s.

The Dachshund (pronounced DAHKS-hund) is a scenthound developed in 16th century Germany to hunt badgers. The name *Dachshund* actually means "badger dog" in German. The badger is a 25 to 40-pound (11 to 18-kg) member of the weasel family with powerful jaws and sharp claws. It is nocturnal and spends its days in underground burrows. Like other scenthounds, Dachshunds hunt in packs so that they can cover a lot of ground quickly when searching for badgers. They bark in excitement while following the scent and "go to ground" after the prey. The Dachshund is perhaps the most extreme of the short-legged and long-bodied hounds. It needed this special build to fit into a badger's burrow. It also needed strong teeth and jaws to pull the tough, fighting badger out of its hole. It was later bred to be a variety of smaller sizes in order to hunt game, such as foxes and rabbits. As pets, these funny little dogs still show some of the hunting behaviors for which they were bred. They love to bark, chase, dig, and burrow under blankets.

What do you call a long, reddish-brown dog? A hot dog, of course! Because of their shape and color, Dachshunds are often called Hot-Dog Dogs or Wiener Dogs.

Basenji

Another scenthound, the Basenji (pronounced buh-SEN-jee) comes from the rainforests of Central Africa. These ancient dogs are called primitive, because they are more like wolves than most dogs. Like wolves, Basenjis don't bark, but they do make other noises, such as howls, yodels, and shrieks. When the dogs hunted the greater cane rat, a local delicacy, their silence helped them to sneak up on the 20-pound (9-kg), long-toothed rodents. Basenjis were trained by pygmy hunters to chase other game, such as wild pig and antelope, into nets. Since the dogs can't bark, they had to wear bells around their necks in order to scare game toward the nets. Basenjis have short, fine hair that keeps them cool in the hot jungle. They wash themselves with their tongues like cats, so their coats stay clean, shiny, and odorless. Because of their hunting instincts, Basenjis, kept as pets, love to play chase and run in the woods.

What kind of name is Basenji?
Basenji is an African word that means "bush thing." *Bush* refers to the thick jungle where the Basenji lives.

Akita

In 17th century Japan, a nobleman moved to the rugged, mountainous island of Honshu, in a territory called Akita (pronounced a-KEE-ta). The nobleman encouraged his samurai to breed a dog powerful enough to hunt bear, deer, and wild boar in the deep snow. The thick-coated, muscular dogs they created were called Akitas, after the territory. The native dog breeds of Japan are very much alike and mainly distinguished by their size. The Akita is the largest. The Japanese love their native breeds so much that they have all been declared national treasures. The Akita is so dedicated to its master, it often doesn't get along well with other animals. It enjoys being an only dog.

Loyal to the end. One Akita named Hachi-Ko greeted his master every night at the train station, until one day the master died at work. The faithful dog continued to wait for his master every evening for the next nine years, until his own death. The story of Hachi-Ko deeply touched the Japanese people. A bronze statue of him now sits at Shibuya Train Station and each year a ceremony is held to celebrate his loyalty.

English Setter

As far back as the 14th century, dogs known as setting spaniels were used to hunt birds in England. They were called setting because of their hunting method, in which they crept toward the hidden birds and then crouched low in a set position. In the 19th century, different breeds of setters began to develop. The English Setter's specialty was locating birds in the flat, spongy wetlands, called moors. The athletic dog ran back and forth in front of the hunter, searching for birds by scent. After the dog set, a net was spread over the entire area, including the dog and the bushes. Then, on command, the dog plunged into the bushes to scare the birds up into the net. The English Setter had to quickly cover a lot of ground when hunting, so it can run for hours. That means that as a pet, it needs lots of exercise to stay healthy.

The fewer, the setter? There are only three breeds of setters: the alert Gordon Setter from Scotland is the heaviest and has a black and tan coat; the playful Irish Setter from Ireland is the tallest and has a solid red coat; and the gentle English Setter is the smallest of the three with a unique flecked coat.

Vizsla

The Vizsla (pronounced VEESH-la) developed from hunting dogs brought to Hungary from Central Asia by the Magyar tribes during the Middle Ages. The fertile plains of Hungary were plentiful with grains, such as wheat, barley, and rye that attracted partridge and other game birds. The Vizsla hunted these birds, locating them by scent and then freezing with a paw raised to point them out to the hunter. The Vizsla, also called the Hungarian Pointer, was well adapted to hunting in this region; its unlimited energy allowed it to hunt all day in the vast fields, while its short coat kept it cool during the long, hot growing season. Vizslas became such prized hunters that they were favorites of wealthy barons and powerful warlords. They were always treated as part of the family so they are extremely affectionate pets. Young Vizslas will sometimes display their hunting instincts by pointing at butterflies and bumblebees.

Golden Vizsla? The Vizsla's coat was once a pale, golden color that helped it blend in with the grassy plains of Hungary. Now, the dog's matching nose, eyes, and coat are rust-colored.

English Cocker Spaniel

Flushing spaniels have been bred as bird hunters in England for hundreds of years. *Flushing* means "scaring the birds into the air." In the late 1800s, hunters divided the spaniels by size. The spaniels under 25 pounds (11 kg) were named Cocker Spaniels after the woodcock, a brown, long-billed game bird they hunted. The larger sizes were called Springer Spaniels and Field Spaniels. The English Cocker Spaniel is a superb hunting dog with a great sense of smell. Its smaller size allows it to go into thick brush to flush out game. It has a soft, wide mouth, which helps it carry birds without damaging them. The Cocker Spaniel is sweet, loyal, and happy. Whether it is on the job hunting, or at home with its family, the Cocker's cheerful personality is shown by its constantly wagging tail.

Can you copy a Cocker? In the 1870s some Cocker Spaniels were brought to the United States from England. For appearance, they were bred to be smaller with rounder heads and longer, silkier hair. The Americanized Cockers are better suited to being pets than hunting companions. Today there are two types of Cockers, the American Cocker Spaniel and the English Cocker Spaniel.

Poodle

Poodles are often thought of as fancy frou-frou dogs, but their ancestors were well established as water retrievers in Germany before the 15th century. The name Poodle comes from the German word *pudel*, which means "to splash." As a bird dog, its hair was cut short in areas so that it could move easily through the water. But the puffball haircut that it is famous for may come from its days as a circus performer, matching the pom-poms worn by the clowns. Because the Poodle was so smart, it quickly learned tricks and loved to perform. It became a favorite dog of French aristocrats and later, it was declared the national dog of France. Poodles make great pets because they are easily trained. They love to imitate people and will often teach themselves to dance or walk on their front feet.

Large, medium or small? The Poodle was bred to be smaller and smaller until it was divided into three groups: the standard, miniature, and toy. The standard Poodle weighs 45 to 65 pounds (20 to 29 kg) and stands 21 inches (53 cm) tall; the miniature weighs 12 to 18 pounds (5 to 8 kg) and stands 10 to 15 inches (25 to 38 cm) tall; the toy Poodle weighs a mere 4 to 8 pounds (1.8 to 3.5 kg) and is under 10 inches (25 cm) tall.

Terriers of Scotland

At one time, all of the terriers from Scotland were thought to be many varieties of one breed. The West Highland White, Scottish, Dandie Dinmont, Cairn, and Skye Terriers probably come from the same ancestor. They are all compact, short-legged, and good at hunting small vermin. However, they were bred in different areas, so each developed unique features and colors. Today they are each thought of as a distinct breed.

The West Highland White comes from the mountainous western coast of Scotland. The "Westie" got its start hunting fox and smaller vermin in the rocky terrain. It is the only white terrier of this group, making it easy to spot in the field. Today, its friendly, playful nature makes it one of the most popular terriers.

The scrappy Scottish Terrier is from the western Scottish Highlands. It is easily recognized by its bushy eyebrows and long, bearded face. A fearless hunter, the "Scottie" worked the farm alone, ridding it of rats, badgers, and foxes by digging them out of the ground and shaking them to death. You can see this kill instinct when a terrier playfully grabs a toy and shakes it.

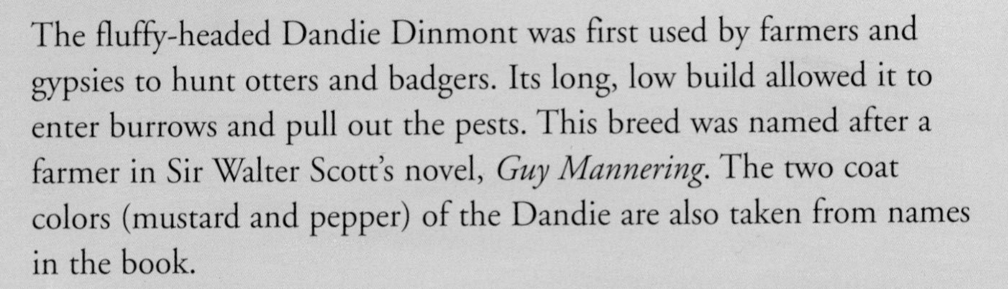

The fluffy-headed Dandie Dinmont was first used by farmers and gypsies to hunt otters and badgers. Its long, low build allowed it to enter burrows and pull out the pests. This breed was named after a farmer in Sir Walter Scott's novel, *Guy Mannering*. The two coat colors (mustard and pepper) of the Dandie are also taken from names in the book.

In Scotland, borders and graves were marked with piles of stones, called cairns. Vermin often made their homes in these cairns. It was the job of the feisty Cairn Terrier to flush the animals out and kill them. Cairn Terriers love to dig with their strong nails in search of pests.

The Skye Terrier gets its name from the Scottish Isle of Skye, where it developed. It is the only terrier of this group to have a long, silky coat. Its coat parts down the middle and even spills over its ears and face. The Skye Terrier is a fierce rodent hunter, but it is also a calm and reserved house pet.

SKYE TERRIER

WEST HIGHLAND WHITE TERRIER

SCOTTISH TERRIER

Parson Jack Russell Terrier

As fox hunting became a gentleman's sport, some terriers were bred to chase foxes out of their dens rather than to kill them. Parson Jack Russell spent sixty-four years developing a fox terrier in England in the 1800s. The Parson favored a rough-coated dog, though smooth-coated fox terriers were more popular at the time. Fox terriers had always been black or red, but the Parson wanted his to be mainly white, so they would be easy to see on the hunt. Parson Jack Russell Terriers' long legs helped them to keep up with riders on horseback and the Foxhounds that were used to locate the fox. Slender and small enough to follow a red fox into its den, they drove the fox out so that the chase could continue. Parson Jack Russell Terriers thrive on adventure and can get into trouble when exploring on their own – they have been known to climb into holes that they have to be rescued from!

A star is born! The smart and adventurous Parson Jack Russell Terrier has been the star of many popular movies and television shows, such as Skip in *My Dog Skip* and the clever dog detective in *Wishbone*.

Herding Breeds

For thousands of years, dogs have been helping people to herd and protect valuable livestock. Some breeds work as *flock guards*, protecting sheep or goats from thieves and predators. These dogs usually grow up with the flock so they will protect them as they would their pack.

THE KOMONDOR, A FLOCK GUARD DOG.

THE BORDER COLLIE, A SHEEP HERDER.

Herding dogs use their hunting instincts to move sheep from place to place. When wolves hunt, they separate certain animals from the herd by stalking, staring, circling, and chasing. Herding dogs use the same techniques to move the sheep in and out of pens, keep the flock together, or separate individual sheep from the flock. Most sheep herding dogs look different than the sheep so that the shepherd can easily spot them.

Drover dogs are breeds that work with cattle. They move these enormous animals out to graze in the pasture or to market. Droving breeds have different methods of getting the cattle to move, but all are good at avoiding the kick of an angry cow's hooves.

THE AUSTRALIAN CATTLE DOG, A CATTLE DROVER.

Some breeds are experts at more than one of these jobs, while some were raised to herd specific animals, such as reindeer. Herding dogs come in many shapes and sizes, but one thing they have in common is tough, all-weather coats that protect them through the harsh weather. These breeds also share the energy and strength to run and work over vast distances for long periods of time.

THE SAMOYED, A REINDEER HERDER.

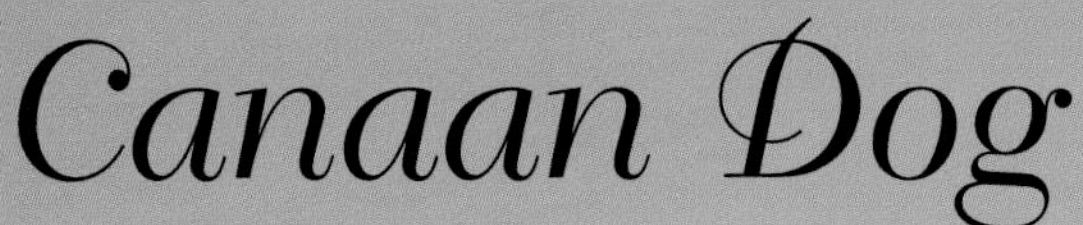

Canaan Dog

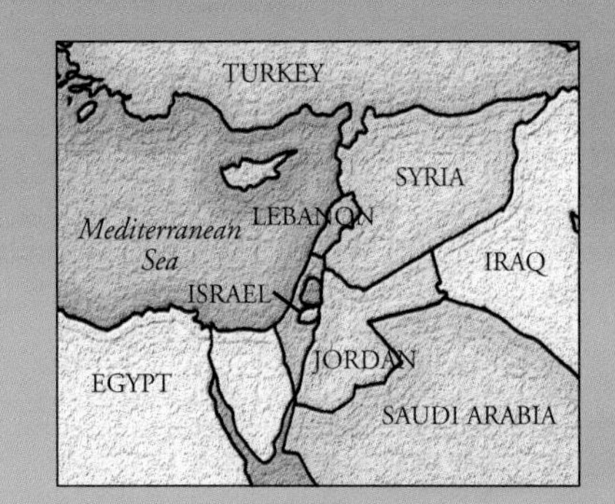

The Canaan (pronounced KAY-nen) Dog was domesticated by the ancient Israelites, as far back as 2000 BC. The dogs herded sheep and goats, and guarded the flocks from jackals and thieves. When Romans forced the Israelites to leave their homeland two thousand years ago, Canaan Dogs fled to the desert. There, they lived on their own for centuries, occasionally being captured for use as herding dogs by the nomadic Bedouin shepherds. In the 20th century, some wild Canaan Dogs were tamed by modern Israelis and trained to serve in the military as guards and messengers, and to sniff out deadly land mines. Today, most of the dogs used by the Israeli army are Canaan Dogs. They can also be found guarding homes, assisting the blind, herding flocks, or still living wild in the desert. They are natural guardians, protective of their families.

Man's best feral *friend?* A *feral* dog is one that was once tame and then returned to life in the wild. In 1934, doctor Rudolphina Menzel was hired by Israel's defense force to train dogs to fight in the Israeli War of Independence. She chose feral Canaan Dogs because they had survived living in the harsh desert for hundreds of years. Because of its dedicated service, the Canaan Dog is now the national dog of Israel.

Puli

Do you brush your hair every day? The Puli doesn't! The Puli and Komondor's thick coats are made by the woolly undercoat tangling with the topcoat. A person then has to separate the hair with their hands into sections to form cords.

Magyar tribesman brought the Puli (pronounced POO-lee) from central Asia to Hungary over a thousand years ago. Since that time, nomadic shepherds of the Hungarian plains have used them to herd *racka*, the native sheep. They were such valuable workers, shepherds sometimes paid up to a year's wages for a Puli. Like other herding dogs, the Puli uses its hunting instincts to move the sheep, but it will never harm them. The Puli has a unique trick to keep its flock in line: if it needs to get to the other side of them quickly, it will jump on top of the sheep and run across their backs. The Puli's thick, corded coat keeps it dry and warm in any kind of weather. As a pet, a Puli's coat needs lots of attention. It can take up to two days to dry after a bath. The hair can be clipped short, but then the dog loses much of its character.

Komondor

The Komondor (pronounced KOM-on-door) developed from large Russian dogs, called Aftscharkas that were brought to Hungary by the Huns. Like the Puli, the Komondor was kept by nomadic Magyar shepherds. But Komondorok (plural for Komondor) performed a different job for the shepherds. They kept the flock safe from predators and thieves, especially at night. Where the Pulik (plural for Puli) are usually black so that the shepherd can see them against the mostly white sheep, Komondorok are white to disguise the dog from predators. This way, an attacker won't know which animal is the one to avoid. Also, the shepherd will never mistake his guard dog for a predator if it blends in with the flock. The Komondor's thick, corded coat protected it not only from the weather, but also from the sharp teeth and claws of attackers. Komondorok had to be brave and independent to work when the shepherd wasn't around. This means that as pets, they might not always follow orders – they prefer to make their own decisions.

Peekaboo, I see you! Even though you can't see the Komondor's eyes, it can see you. Looking out through cords of hair is like looking through mini-blinds.

Border Collie

The Border Collie was developed in the 1800s along the borders of England, Scotland, and Wales. It is known for being one of the smartest breeds of dogs. It works by listening to its master's whistles and calls. Like a wolf separating an animal from its herd, the Border Collie reads a sheep's body movements and silently intimidates it into running in a certain direction. "Giving eye" is a method of staring that Border Collies use while stalking sheep until they move. It is the Border Collie's specialty. The Border Collie, still a popular farm worker, is one of the few breeds that is bred more for its working ability than its appearance. Because they are so smart and have boundless energy, Border Collies need to be exercised physically and mentally every day.

Flyball, anyone? Some dogs and their owners compete together in sports such as flyball. In flyball, teams of four dogs run a relay race by jumping over hurdles, pushing a box that releases a ball, then catching the ball and running to the finish line. The Border Collie is so quick and agile, it is a champion of the sport.

Bearded Collie

The black sheep of Scotland were named *colly*, meaning "like coal," and the dogs used to herd them took that name as well. The Bearded Collie is one such dog. It has a long, flat coat, with hair growing from its cheeks, lower lip, and chin to form a beard. The "Beardie" worked in the Scottish Highlands where its shaggy coat protected it from the cold, damp weather. Its sturdy build and large, well-padded feet helped it run over the rocky terrain. It is thought that the Beardie came to Scotland several hundred years ago from Central Europe. It may have been the offspring of Komondors. It worked both as a sheepherder and cattle drover. The Beardie was such a valuable worker that the shepherds didn't want to sell any of the puppies unless they would be put to work. As a pet, the energetic and playful Bearded Collie is always eager to romp outside, thanks to its protective coat.

Fading fast? Beardies are born black, brown, blue, or fawn, with white markings. By the time they reach age one, their color has usually faded to a much lighter shade. A black pup will probably grow up to be gray and a brown pup will turn tan.

Pembroke Welsh Corgi

'Tis said that long ago in the misty Welsh forest lived a kingdom of magical fairies. Their queen and her fairy warriors needed steeds that could carry them o'er great distances, so they created an enchanted breed of little dogs. One day while the queen was out riding, two of her pups ran into a field, where human farmers were working. She did not go after them for she knew that her magical dogs would be a great help to the poor farmers. The dogs learned to assist the farmers in many ways, as they still do today. 'Tis said that if you look carefully on the shoulders of a Corgi, you can still see the marks left by the wee fairy saddles.

This is the legend of the Pembroke Welsh Corgi, a short-legged, spunky dog from Wales. The name *Corgi* means "dwarf dog" in the Welsh language. Corgis are the smallest of the herding dogs. They move cattle by nipping at their heels. The dogs are low enough to avoid a cow's hoof when it kicks. These fanciful dogs have some fairly unusual behaviors. They have been known to rear up and hop on their short hind legs when they are angry, and with a quick twist when lying on their backs, they can jump up and land right on their feet.

Two kinds of Corgis? Besides the Pembroke, there is also the Cardigan Welsh Corgi. You can tell the two apart by looking at their tails and ears. The Cardigan has rounded ears and a long brushy tail, while the Pembroke has pointed ears and a short tail.

Australian Cattle Dog

During the 1800s, cattle ranchers in Australia began having trouble with the cows they had brought with them from Europe. The cattle had become wild, living in the harsh outback. The European herding dogs could no longer handle the unruly cows. So the ranchers set out to develop a new breed of cattle dog. It had to be able to work in the extreme Australian heat and think on its own when the ranchers weren't around. It also needed to work in a way that didn't frighten the cattle – without barking or rough biting. So the ranchers bred their dogs with the wild Australian Dingo, a quiet and hardy native dog. After many years, the ranchers perfected the Australian Cattle Dog. It is an expert herder, using its bushy tail to balance, while making sharp turns to stay with the cattle. It nips at their heels to move them and then instantly flattens out on the ground to avoid a kick. Its instincts have led the Australian Cattle Dog to sometimes nip at its family members in an attempt to herd them.

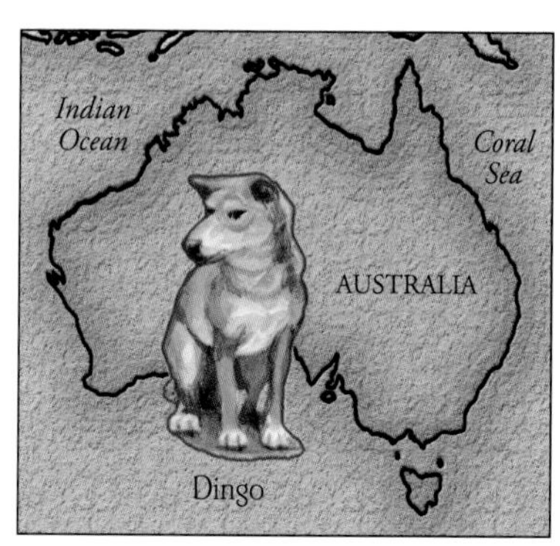

Dog or Dingo? The Australian Dingo is a breed of dog that migrated to Australia with the Aborigines thousands of years ago. Today's Dingoes are feral, living wild in the outback. They look like tame dogs, but behave more like wolves.

Samoyed

Samoyeds (pronounced SAM-oy-eds) are from Siberia, a vast frozen land in the far north of Russia. They belong to the spitz family of dogs. Most spitz dogs were multi-purpose working breeds, but Samoyeds were mainly used for herding. They were trained to herd the hundreds of reindeer that the nomadic Samoyede people depended on. The reindeer, in turn, did most of the work pulling sleds and boats. Reindeer meat provided food, and their hides were used for clothing, huts, and beds. Samoyeds also guarded the reindeer from wolves and bears. The deer had to roam over a huge area in order to find the sparse moss on which they grazed. This made herding and guarding them much more challenging. The wooly dogs lived in the deerskin huts and kept their families warm at night. As a pet, the Samoyed's instincts may inspire it to explore many miles from home and to herd the neighborhood squirrels, rabbits, and cats.

What makes Samoyeds look so happy? The joyful Samoyed has dark lips that curve up at the corners to create what's known as the "Sammy" smile.

Working Breeds

Working dogs are breeds that do types of work other than hunting and herding. They need to be large and strong to complete their difficult jobs. Some of the oldest working breeds are of the *spitz* type. Dogs in this family have upright triangular ears, thick fur, and a bushy curled tail. Spitz-type dogs were developed for work in the frozen Arctic region (the land areas near the North Pole). Most spitz dogs are hardworking, multi-purpose dogs. One of their main jobs was draughting – pulling heavy loads such as sleds or boats.

The Chow Chow, a spitz-type dog.

The Greater Swiss Mountain Dog, a draught dog.

Other breeds of *draught dogs* were developed to pull carts of dairy or produce around farms and to market. In addition to pulling the cart, a draught dog was often responsible for protecting the cart's contents.

The Doberman Pinscher, a guard dog.

Some dogs were bred to work as *guard dogs*. This job comes naturally because all dogs are territorial and instinctively protect their pack. Successful guard dogs have the size and muscle to protect their master and his property. They also bark, unlike wolves, to warn intruders away.

The English Bulldog, a fighting breed.

Another job dogs were bred to do is fight. Some *fighting breeds* followed their masters into battle, while others were trained from an early age to fight for the entertainment of people. These dogs were bred to have special builds and aggressive personalities.

One of the more unusual jobs for working breeds was that of the *water dog*. These breeds assisted fisherman in many ways and rescued people from rough seas. They had warm, waterproof coats and webbed feet.

The Portuguese Water Dog, a water breed.

Alaskan Malamute

The Alaskan Malamute is named after the Mahlemut tribe that raised the breed on Alaska's northwest coast. It is the largest, strongest, and possibly the oldest of the Arctic sled dogs. Because it is so strong and solid, one Malamute can do the work of many smaller sled dogs. These dogs were essential to the Mahlemut people for moving their belongings from place to place, and for hunting seals and polar bears. The hunters relied on their dogs to haul the heavy animal carcasses home and trusted the dogs with their lives on the dangerous ice. Malamute dogs were so important to the Mahlemut tribe, they were treated like members of the family. That is why today, the Malamute is the friendliest and most affectionate variety of sled dog. A Malamute as a pet needs to be trained how to walk properly on a leash, or it will pull its owner down the block as if it is pulling a sled through Alaska.

How strong do you have to be to pull a polar bear? In weight-pulling competitions, a single Malamute will sometimes pull over 3,000 pounds (1.3 tonnes). That's thirty-seven times its own weight – and over twice the weight of a polar bear!

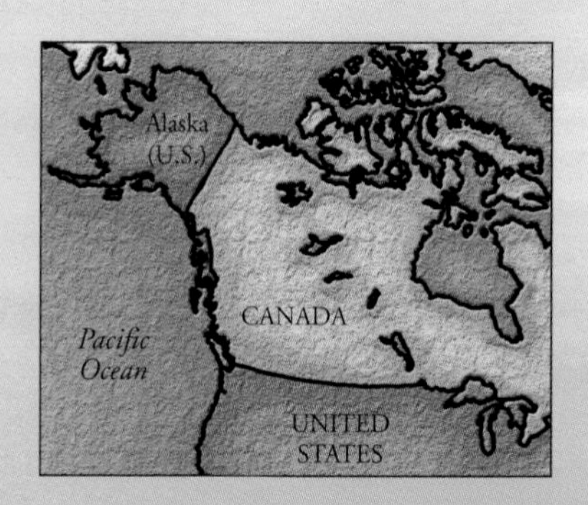

Chow Chow

Before there were stars in the heavens, there was Earth. And on Earth there lived Chow Chow dogs. They looked much like other dogs, with fluffy warm coats, pink tongues, and tails that curled over their backs. Then the stars were chiseled into the heavens, which caused bits of sky to fall to Earth. The Chow Chows lapped up the blue-black sky as it fell, and their wide tongues became the color of the heavens.

This Chinese legend explains how the Chow Chow's tongue came to be blue-black in color. The Chinese began breeding Chows over two thousand years ago to guard homes and temples. It was thought that their dark mouths scared away evil spirits when they barked. They were also used for pulling carts and as a source of food and fur. As former guard dogs, Chows are very loyal and protective of their owners. They tend to be one-person dogs.

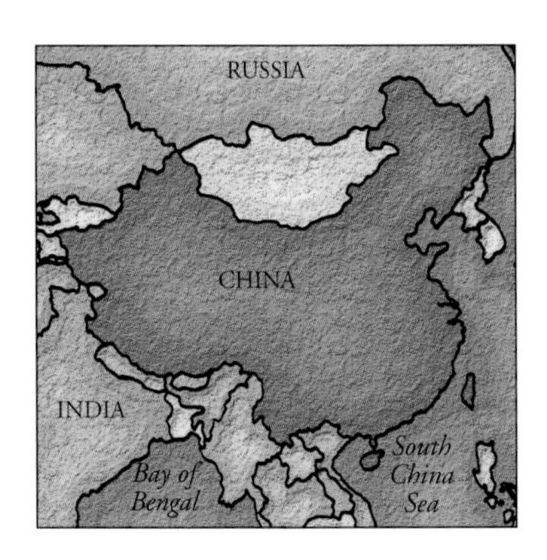

Have you ever gone out to get some chow? The Chow Chow's name may have come from a Chinese word meaning "food," since the dogs were frequently a menu item. More likely though, they were named by British sailors in the late 1700s after a term for Chinese knick-knacks.

Sennenhunds

When Roman soldiers invaded mountainous Switzerland in the first century BC, they brought large mastiff-type guard dogs with them. These Roman dogs mixed with native herding dogs to create the *Sennenhunds*, or "Swiss Mountain Dogs." Sennenhunds are broad and strong like mastiffs, yet gentle and able to withstand cold

weather like native Swiss dogs. They worked many jobs on farms in the sloping valleys of the lower Alps. These four breeds of mountain dogs, the Greater Swiss, Bernese, Entelbuch, and Appenzell, share a common coat pattern of black, white, and rust, but they are different in other ways.

The Greater Swiss Mountain Dog is the largest Sennenhund. At over 130 pounds (59 kg), the "Swissie" was sometimes called the poor man's horse. They worked as hard as horses, pulling carts of produce to market, but didn't eat nearly as much.

The Bernese Mountain Dog is the only Sennenhund to have long silky fur, which helps it to withstand the cold Alpine weather. It was an all-purpose farmworker and patiently pulled carts of flowers, baskets, milk, and cheese to market. Its strong neck, broad chest, and muscular back legs made it good at hauling heavy loads.

The Entelbuch Mountain Dog is the shortest Sennenhund and has a bobtail. It was used mainly to drive cattle to market. The small, energetic Entelbuch used to jump up and hurl its body at the much larger cattle to move them, and will sometimes still do that to its family during play.

ENTELBUCH MOUNTAIN DOG

At 49 to 55 pounds (22 to 25 kg), the Appenzell Mountain Dog is the lightest Sennenhund, with a tail that curls up over its back. This Sennenhund, in addition to carting dairy to the market, herded goats in the mountains. It needed to be light, swift, and sure-footed to follow the goats over rocky terrain.

GREATER SWISS MOUNTAIN DOG

Saint Bernard

The Saint Bernard Hospice was a shelter for travelers who crossed the steep snow-covered mountains between Switzerland and Italy. Large farm dogs were first brought to the hospice around 1660 to guard and pull carts for the monks. Soon after that, the monks realized that these dogs had more valuable skills. They were experts at finding their way through deep snow. With their sensitive hearing and keen sense of smell, they were able to locate travelers who became trapped in deadly avalanches and blizzards. When the St. Bernard dog found a person in the snow, it licked him in the face to wake him, snuggled close to warm him, and barked to alert the monks. The dogs were later named Saint Bernards after the hospice because of the lifesaving work they did there. The good-natured Saint Bernard makes a calm and gentle pet. It prefers cold climates because it was bred to work in the snow.

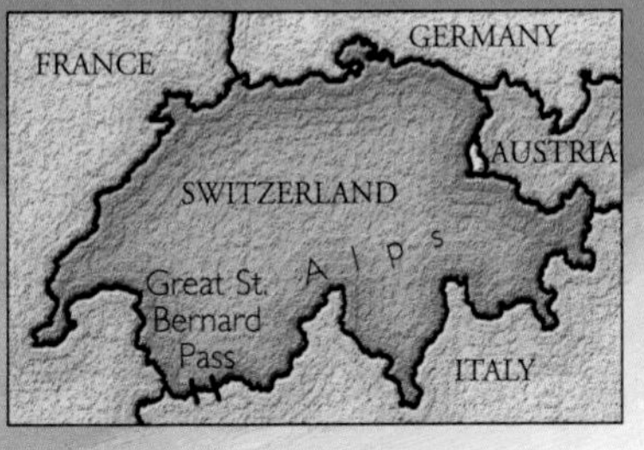

Is the Saint Bernard a superhero? In the three centuries that the dogs have worked at the Saint Bernard Hospice, they have rescued over two thousand people. The most famous Saint Bernard, Barry, lived at the monastery from 1800 to 1812. He alone saved forty lives.

Dalmatian

The spotted Dalmatian is an ancient breed. It gets its name from Dalmatia (now known as western Croatia) where it had many jobs, such as guarding and hunting. In Victorian England it became the one and only *Carriage Dog.* It tirelessly ran for miles underneath, beside, or behind its master's carriage. It not only added a decorative accent to the fancy carriage, but also protected passengers from stray dogs and highway robbers along the way. Dalmatians naturally protected the horses as they would their pack, because the animals were raised together. As modern cars replaced horse-drawn carriages, Dalmatians became less popular. They still ran with horse-drawn fire engines, so they became known as Firehouse Dogs. Today, there are no horse-drawn vehicles for the dogs to protect, but Dalmatians still get along well with horses and love to run. Because they are so athletic, Dalmatians make excellent jogging companions.

Can a dog change its spots?
Dalmatian puppies are born solid white and develop their famous round spots when they are about two or three weeks old. The Dalmatian's spots can be either black or liver-colored.

Doberman Pinscher

The fearless Doberman Pinscher (pronounced PIN-sher) was developed in Germany in 1890 by a man named Ludwig Dobermann. He wanted a strong, brave dog to protect him from thieves and angry taxpayers, while he worked as a door-to-door tax collector. He also wanted the dog to be smart, easily trained, and easy to take care of. Mr. Dobermann ran the local dog pound, so he knew which dogs to breed to get the features that he wanted. Today, Doberman Pinschers are known for their intelligence, energy, and athletic ability. They have served as police, war, and criminal-trailing dogs. Thanks to Mr. Dobermann, the Doberman Pinscher is excellent in obedience training, a great family protector, and its short coat needs almost no grooming.

Army, navy, or air force? Dogs have assisted the military in wars around the world for centuries. In World War II, more than a thousand Doberman Pinschers served as United States Marine Corps "Devil Dogs" in the Pacific. They acted as guards, messengers, and scouts, explored jungles and caves, and detected mines, booby traps, and snipers.

Neapolitan Mastiff

In 300 BC, Alexander the Great brought a massive war dog called the Molossus to Rome from the Middle East. The Neapolitan Mastiff developed from this dog. It is still a colossal breed, sometimes weighing over 150 pounds (68 kg). With their large, broad heads and heavy bones, Neapolitans were built for fighting. In ancient Rome, they were used as gladiator dogs (dogs that fought with people or wild animals in the arena for the audience's entertainment), and are said to have fought fiercely in wars alongside Roman Emperor Caesar. These dogs were also popular watchdogs because of their size, strength, and frightening appearance. Today's Neapolitan Mastiff makes a gentle, loving family pet. Though it is no longer an aggressive war dog, it enjoys a game of tug-of-war in the yard now and then.

Would you play hide and seek with a Neapolitan Mastiff? These tough looking dogs come in a variety of colors, but bluish-gray has always been the most popular. A dog this color can easily hide in the shadows and blend into the darkness of night.

English Bulldog

In the 1200s, the English Bulldog was bred in the British Isles for a violent sport called bullbaiting. In bullbaiting, several dogs attacked a chained bull, usually targeting its sensitive nose. The Bulldog's strong wide jaws clamped onto the bull, while its pushed back nose allowed it to keep breathing. The dog could crouch down low to avoid the bull's horns because its legs were set far apart. Its muscular front end gave it the strength to spring up and attack the bull, while its light back end meant that its spine was less likely to be injured when it was being shaken. Still, Bulldogs were often injured or killed during fights. In 1835, the cruel sport of bullbaiting was outlawed. The fierce Bulldog was then bred to be a companion. Over generations it became gentle and friendly. It is now a well-loved pet and a national symbol of England.

Who was known as the "Bulldog of Britain"? It was Sir Winston Churchill, England's famous prime minister during World War II. Like the Bulldog, he was courageous and stubborn and never gave up. If you look closely at a photo of Churchill, you might even think he looks like a Bulldog.

Boxer

Is plastic surgery for the dogs? Many breeds, including the Boxer, traditionally have their ears *cropped* and their tails *docked*. Cropping is cutting off part of the ears so that they will stand upright. Docking is cutting the tail very short. Today, these procedures are done simply for appearance. Cropping and docking have been outlawed in many countries because they serve no purpose and are painful for the dogs.

The Boxer was developed in Germany in the 1800s. It is part mastiff-type dog (which gave it its size and muscular build), and part Bulldog (which gave it its short nose and square head). Like other relatives of the Bulldog, the Boxer was used for dogfighting and bullbaiting until the sports were outlawed in the mid-19th century. The name *Boxer* comes from the way the dogs fight with their front paws (like men boxing). The Boxer is very smart. That is why it was one of the first breeds used in Germany as a police dog and a guide dog. As a pet, its intelligence can lead it to be mischievous when left alone and bored. Boxers are friendly, playful, and affectionate dogs.

A Boxer with natural ears and tail.

Portuguese Water Dog

The Portuguese Water Dog began working for fishermen in Portugal in the Middle Ages. It worked off of fishing boats, not only in the warm waters of Portugal, but also in the frigid waters of faraway Iceland. Its webbed feet helped it to swim messages between boats and to the shore, herd fish into nets, and carry nets and buoys in the water. By the 1930s, Portuguese fishermen began to use radios to send messages and winches to pull in nets. These modern inventions meant that the dogs were no longer essential on fishing boats. The "Portie" was in danger of dying out, but it has now become a popular family pet. It enjoys sharing every family activity. It is said that having to endure daily hardships encountered by the Portuguese fisherman has prepared the Portie to withstand any fate that comes, even the most wild and playful of children.

Dog for hire? Before modern fishing methods, Portuguese Water Dogs were extremely valuable workers on fishing boats. Retired fishermen sometimes rented out their dogs for money. The dogs themselves were paid in fish.

Newfoundland

The giant Newfoundland (pronounced new-fun-LAND) gets its name from the Canadian island where it was developed in the 1700s. Its ancestors were brought to the island by European fishermen. The Newfoundland is perfect for the area's long, cold winters and icy waters. It has a heavy, oily coat and strong, webbed feet, which make it an excellent swimmer. The "Newf" could do almost any kind of work in the water. The dogs carried rescue lines to wrecked ships, towed lifeboats to shore, saved people from drowning in the rough sea, and helped fishermen with their nets. Newfs are still used as working dogs today, but even as pets, they love to swim and pull things. They make great playmates and protectors for children because of their sweet, gentle, and patient personalities.

Newfound friends? When famous adventurers Lewis and Clark set out to explore lands west of the Mississippi River, they brought with them Lewis' Newfoundland, Seaman. Seaman hunted and protected the camp, but his most valuable job was to greet Native American tribes with guide and translator, Sacagawea. The natives had never seen such a large and powerful, yet gentle dog. They often asked Lewis to trade his Newfoundland for beaver skins.

The Labrador Retriever also comes from Newfoundland, Canada. In the 1800s it was known as the Lesser Newfoundland because it was a smaller, shorthaired version of the mighty Newfoundland. Like its larger cousin, the Labrador Retriever was used for all sorts of water tasks. It was preferred over the Newf in smaller fishing boats. The "Lab" took up less room and its short, waterproof coat didn't bring much water into the boat. Labs became devoted companions of the fishermen on the Labrador Sea. After years of retrieving fish, it was easy for the Lab to become a skilled bird dog. Today it is considered a sporting breed, best known for its work retrieving ducks from the water after they have been shot. The lovable Lab is currently the most popular dog in North America. Its retrieving skills make it an expert at fetching newspapers, slippers, and toys.

NEWFOUNDLAND & LABRADOR RETRIEVER

Legendary Labrador. In 1959, a black Labrador Retriever named King Buck became the first dog ever to appear on a U.S. postage stamp. The national retriever champion appeared on a migratory bird-hunting stamp to promote the use of retrievers. When hunters use retrieving dogs, fewer birds are lost after they have been shot.

Companion Breeds

Companion dogs are breeds that were created for their ability to live with people, more than their ability to do any type of work. Throughout history, people have wanted different things from their companion dogs. As a result, just as there are different types of hunting, herding, and working breeds, there is also much variety in companion breeds.

The Shih Tzu, designed to resemble the lion that the religious leader Buddha once tamed.

The Papillon, a miniaturized version of popular hunting spaniels.

Some societies bred companion dogs to remind them of their religious leaders, or to provide company in the afterlife. Others bred dogs to provide comfort and warmth. There are companion breeds that kept sailors company on long voyages and were traded for goods in ports. Miniature versions of popular breeds, or *toys*, were designed to be cute and decorative.

In the 19th century, people began to breed dogs as a hobby and wanted companions to compete with in dog shows. In general, companion dogs were bred to have friendly, gentle personalities, delicate and pleasing appearances, and to be small and portable in size.

The Boston Terrier, bred for the show ring.

Although so much emphasis is placed on pure-breeds today, most domestic dogs in the world are still *mixed-breed* animals. Since they are not bred for a specific purpose, they are best known as pets.

A Mixed-Breed dog, a great family companion.

Chihuahua

Since the 5th century, the civilizations of Central America kept little dogs like the Chihuahua (pronounced CHIH-wa-wa): first the Mayans, then the Toltecs, and finally the Aztecs. The Aztecs thought that these dogs, which they called *Techichis*, would guide their souls to the underworld. When an Aztec died, one of their dogs was sacrificed and buried with the deceased person. King Montezuma II kept hundreds of these dome-headed dogs in his palace. In the 1500s, the Spanish explorer Cortés and his conquistadors conquered the Aztec people and used the little dogs as food. Those that survived lived with the few native people who also fled from the Spanish. Some dogs survived on their own in the jungle, eating insects, lizards, and plants. Three hundred years later, the dogs were rediscovered in the ruins of King Montezuma's palace in Chihuahua, Mexico. After spending hundreds of years living alone, the Chihuahua prefers the company of dogs of its own breed and enjoys chasing bugs.

Which weighs more, a dog or a cat? The Chihuahua, the smallest of all dogs, weighs 2 to 6 pounds (1 to 2.7 kg), while the average housecat weighs 7 to 10 pounds (3 to 4.5 kg).

Can a dog tell the future? In the Forbidden City of Peking, a white spot on the top of a Shih Tzu's head was called the eye of Buddha. It was thought that through this "eye" the dog could predict the future.

Shih Tzu

The Shih Tzu (pronounced SHEED-zoo) is best known for its days as a palace dog in China, where it was constantly pampered. It ate meals at the emperor's table, slept on beds of the finest silk and had guards to protect it. The Shih Tzu, or "Little Lion" is one of many dogs in Asia that were bred to look like the lion, an important symbol in the Buddhist religion. So that it would more closely resemble a lion, its flowing hair was trimmed. Each year a contest was held to find the dog that looked most like the Lion of Buddha. Winners had their portraits painted in the emperor's official records and their attendants were given gifts and titles of honor. As a former palace pet, the Shih Tzu is gentle, sweet, and playful, but it also needs lots of grooming. Like human hair, the Shih Tzu's luxurious hair continually grows.

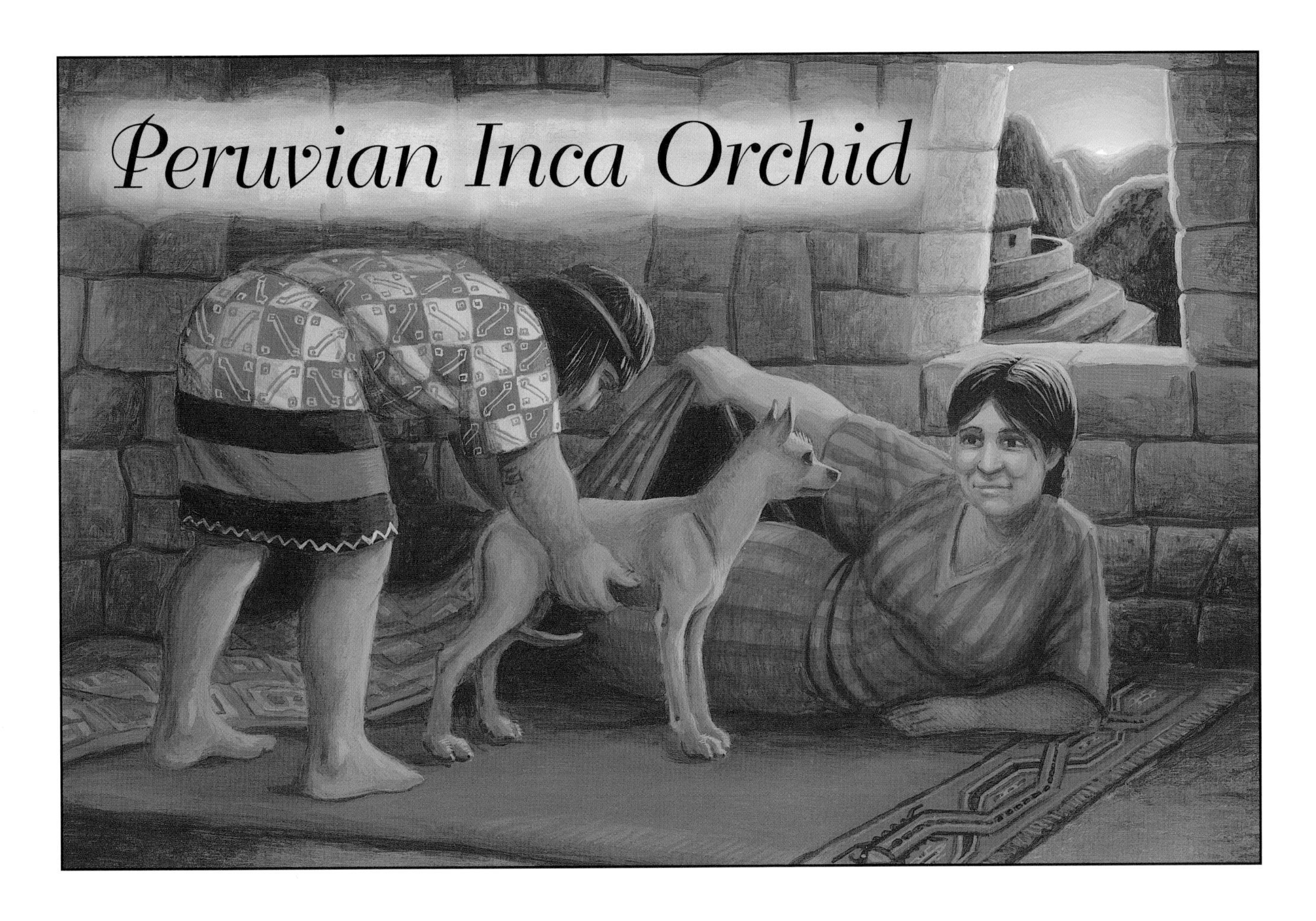

The hairless Peruvian Inca Orchid was kept by the Inca Indians in the mountains of ancient Peru. The dogs lived with the nobility as companions and bed warmers. They were well suited for these roles because their lack of hair kept the dogs from smelling bad and getting fleas. The dogs were also used to soothe aches and pains from arthritis or other illnesses. Their bare bodies felt like hot water bottles to the Incans because dogs have a higher body temperature than humans. Even though they are "hairless," they actually have fine hair on top of their heads, feet, and the tips of their tails. The Peruvian Inca Orchid has delicate pink skin, usually with a dark spotted pattern. As pets, these naked dogs need protection from the sun by wearing sunscreen and from the cold by wearing sweaters.

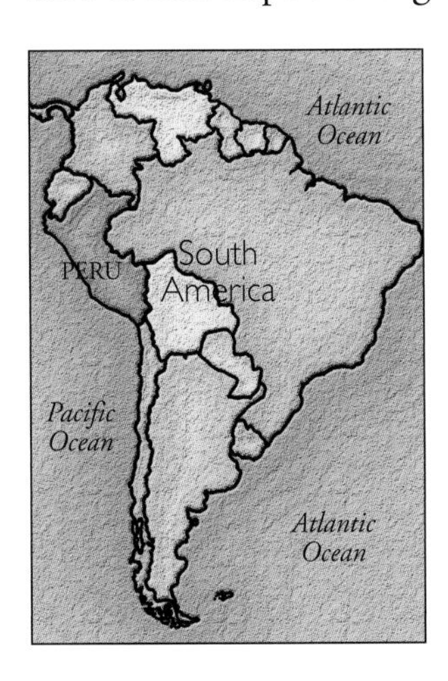

Are there dogs growing in your garden? When the Spanish conquered Peru in the early 1500s, they found these dogs amongst the Incans' beautiful orchid plants. That is why today the breed is called Peruvian Inca Orchid.

Bichon Frisé

In ancient times, Spanish sailors brought water spaniels from the Mediterranean and traded them to the people of the Canary Islands. The curly-haired Bichon Frisé (pronounced BEE-shon Free-ZAY) developed from these dogs. In the 14th century, Italian sailors exported them back to the European continent. They quickly became favorite pets of the upper class and royalty. Bichons could be found pampered in ribbons and perfume in the French court and modeling for famous painters in Spain. By the late 19th century though, the breed lost popularity. Bichons became common street dogs. Their intelligence and perky personalities earned them their meals, as they performed for crowds. The Bichon Frisé was bred to have a puppy-like personality, so it remains playful throughout its life and loves to learn tricks.

Would you trade your pooch for pineapples? Long ago it was common for sailors to exchange dogs for goods. This is how dogs in the Bichon family spread to many different islands. Malta's Maltese, Cuba's Havanese, and Madagascar's Coton de Tulear, are all related to the Bichon Frisé.

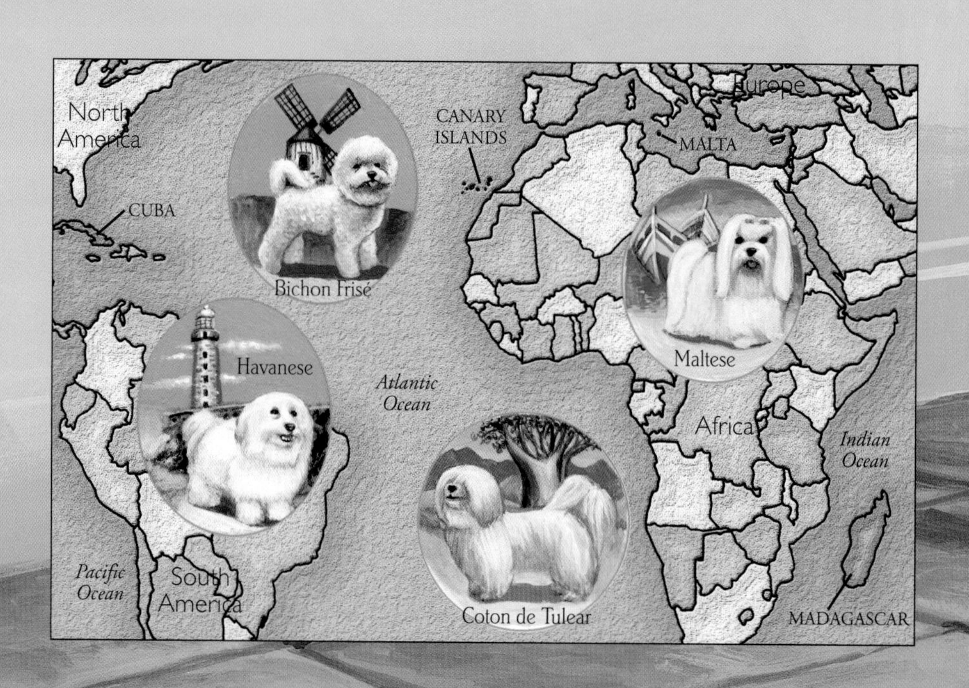

Papillon

The Papillon (pronounced PAPPY-yon) was bred from dwarf spaniels in the 16th century. It was developed and traded by European aristocrats in Spain, Italy, and France. The word *papillon* is French for "butterfly." This name describes the shape made by the dog's fringed ears and facial markings. Originally, their large ears were folded down, but at some point in the breed's history the ears began to stand up. Today, it is common to find dogs with upright ears and with drooping ears in the same litter. The droop-eared variety is called *Phalene* (pronounced FAY-lean), which is French for "moth." Until a puppy is around eight to ten weeks old, it is impossible to tell if it will be a Papillon or Phalene – as it matures, its ears will begin to stand up if it is a Papillon. These obedient toy dogs are gentle, shy, and playful.

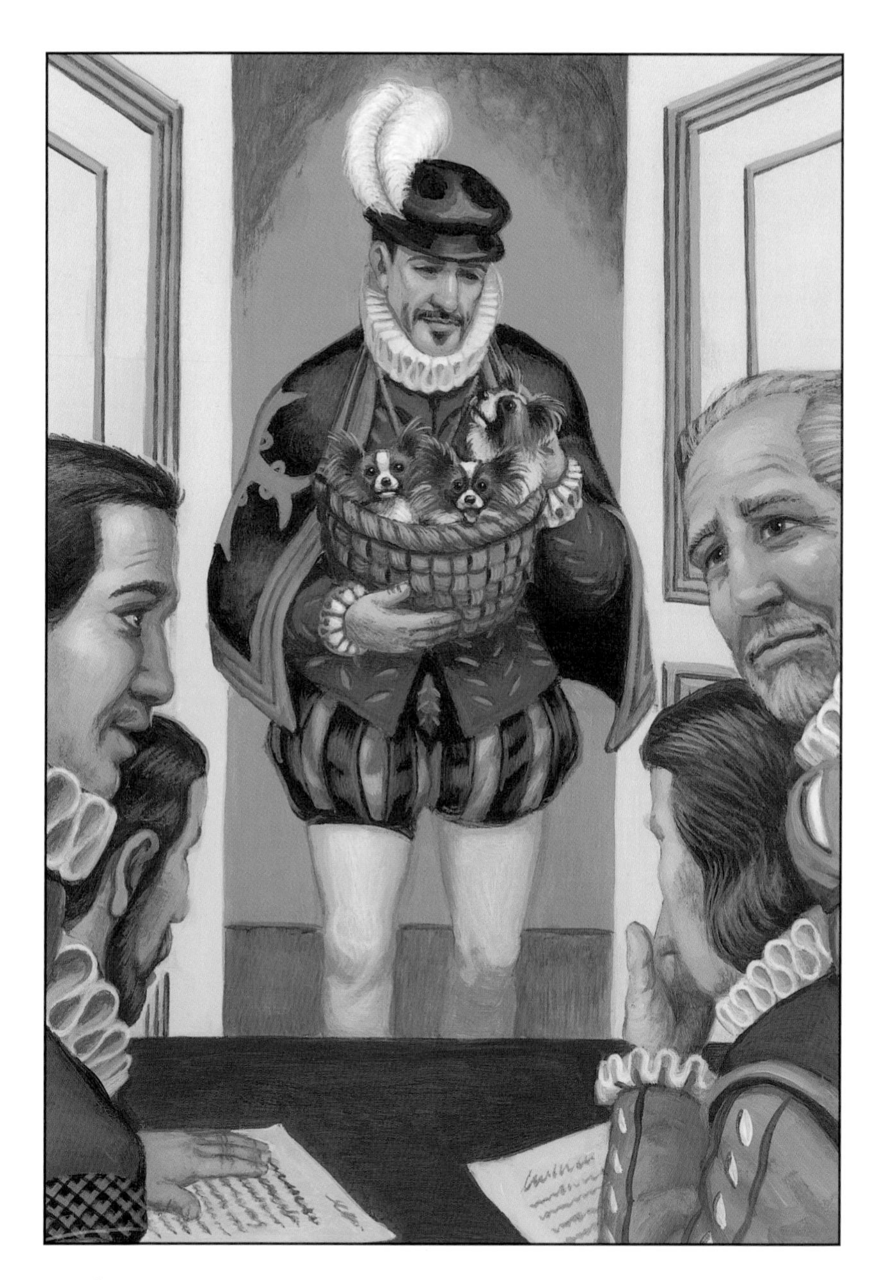

Is it bring-your-dog-to-work day? French King Henry III often attended official meetings with a basket full of Papillons around his neck. He was sometimes accused of ignoring matters of state because he was too busy playing with his dogs.

Phalene & Papillon

An orange dog? In 1572, Dutch Prince William of Orange's faithful Pug, Pompey, saved him from a night attack. After that, the Pug became the official dog of the prince's family, the House of Orange.

Pug

The Pug is thought to have been developed before 400 BC. It is one of many ancient breeds that were miniaturized in Asia. The Pug is possibly the only toy breed that is a direct descendant of mastiff-type dogs. Dogs in the mastiff family are usually big and strong, with large heads and short muzzles. Many of them are used for fighting or protection, but the Pug is better known as a clownish companion. It was a favorite pet in Buddhist monasteries of Tibet and prized for its facial wrinkles in China. To the Chinese, the Pug's most important wrinkle was in the center of the forehead. It was called the *prince mark* because it resembles the Chinese character for "prince." The short sinuses in this flat-faced breed often cause it to make snorting sounds as it breathes. Almost every pug snores when sleeping.

In 1865, the coachmen who worked for Boston's wealthy class began crossbreeding some of their employer's purebred dogs. It all began with Robert C. Hooper's dog, Judge. Judge was a cross between an English Bulldog and a white English Terrier. The men carefully selected a small white female dog with a short tail to mate with Judge. Then their son was bred to another dog that the men had chosen. The process continued until a new breed was born. Boston Terriers have blocky heads like the Bulldog with terrier-like bodies. Their ears are upright, eyes wide-set, and tails short. They are either black or brindle (vertical bands of dark and light hair) with white markings around the muzzle, between the eyes, and on the chest. Unlike most terriers that were bred to hunt vermin, the Boston Terrier was bred for the show ring. It quickly became a popular companion and show dog in the United States. It is sometimes called The American Gentleman because it is so charming and gentle. It loves learning tricks and is wonderful with children.

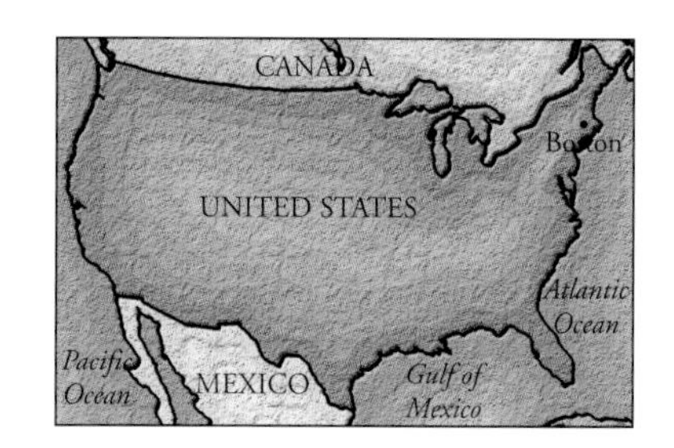

Who are you calling Round Head? Round Head was the original name for the breed. In 1891, the dogs were officially named Boston Terriers after their birthplace.

Mixed-Breed

Dogs within a particular breed tend to look and act the same. The puppies will always look like their parents. In most cases, humans have played a part in creating the breed by selecting which dogs should mate. They have even written rules or standards that dictate exactly how dogs of that breed should look and behave. A mixed-breed dog is the opposite. Its parents were different breeds from each other, or mixed-breed dogs themselves. A mixed-breed dog can look like one of its parents or have a combination of its parents' features. They can be just as smart, loving, and playful as purebred dogs. There are currently more mixed-breed dogs living in North American homes than purebred dogs.

To breed or not to breed? When breeders see traits that they like in a family of dogs, they will often breed those dogs to each other. Because the parents are closely related, they will share not only good traits, but also bad traits. As a result, the parents can easily pass diseases or genetic health problems down to their puppies. This is why mixed-breed dogs are often healthier than purebred dogs. There is less chance that both of the dog's parents have a trait for the same disease or health problem.

Conclusion

Usually, the first thing you notice about a dog is the way it looks. There is so much variety in the dog world – dogs can be short-legged or long-legged, muscular or slender, long-nosed or flat-faced, and so many different colors! But each breed also has its own unique behaviors. Today, most breeds are companion dogs; very few actually do the work they were originally meant to do. Hopefully now, you have a better idea of why some dogs like to dig, play chase, swim, or even sleep in your bed. If you are thinking of getting a dog, do more research first. Will you be able to give this dog as much activity and exercise as its breed needs to stay healthy? Think about what you want from your pet. Are you interested in showing, working, or breeding your dog? If not, consider a mixed-breed dog. If you are just looking for a playful companion, adopting a dog from a local shelter or rescue organization is a good option. Most breeds have groups that are devoted to rescuing that breed of dog. Every dog, whether pure- or mixed-breed, has its own special qualities and quirks, even though they all share the same ancestor – the wolf.

Bibliography

Adamson, Eve. "Pointing the Way: Vizsla." *Dog Fancy*, January 2003, 52-55.

"Shih Tzu: Courtly Companion." *Dog Fancy*, January 2003, 46-51.

"Tough Act to Follow: Bulldog." *Dog Fancy*, July 2004, 46-51.

Alderton, David. *Dogs*. New York: Dorling Kindersley, 1993.

Allan-Scott, Lesley. *The English Setter*. Great Britain: Popular Dogs Publishing Co., Ltd., 1989.

American Kennel Club. *The Complete Dog Book*. New York: Howell Book House, 1998.

Animal Planet. *Breed All About It: Australian Cattle Dog*. Animal Planet, 2002.

Breed All About It: Chow Chow. Animal Planet, 2002.

Breed All About It: Rhodesian Ridgeback. Animal Planet, 2002.

Breed All About It: Saluki. Animal Planet, 2002.

Atkinson, James B. *Chow Chows*. New York: Barron's Educational Series, 1988.

Braund, Kathryn. *The New Complete Portuguese Water Dog*. USA: Howell Book House, 1997.

Bush, Keith. "American Spirit: Boston Terrier." *Dog Fancy*, July 2004, 30.

Caddy, George. *Cocker Spaniel (English)*. USA: T.F.H. Publications, Inc., 1993.

Clutton-Brock, Juliet. *Eyewitness Books: Dog*. New York: Dorling Kindersley, 1991.

Coile, D. Caroline. *Encyclopedia of Dog Breeds*. New York: Barron's Educational Series, 1998.

Coren, Stanley. *The Pawprints of History: Dogs and the Course of Human Events*. New York: Free Press, 2002.

Davis, Tom. *Why Dogs Do That: A Collection of Curious Canine Behaviors*. Wisconsin: Willow Creek Press, 1998.

Derr, Mark. "Collie or Pug? Study Finds the Genetic Code." *New York Times*, 21 May 2004.

Fogle, Bruce. *ASPCA: Complete Dog Care Manual*. New York: Dorling Kindersley, 1993.

Fogle, Bruce. *Dog Breed Handbooks: Dachshund*. New York: Dorling Kindersley, 1999.

Grounds, Beryl and Geoff. *All About the Samoyed*. England: Kingdom Books, 1998.

Jackson, Jean and Frank. *Parson Jack Russell Terriers*. England: The Crowood Press, 1999.

Kikuchi, June. "Breed Files." *Dogs for Kids*, Summer 2004, 19-23.

Kojima, Toyoharu. *Legacy of the Dog*. San Francisco: Chronicle Books, 1993.

Kopatch, L.J. Kip. *The Complete Chow Chow*. USA: Howell Book House, 1988.

Michael D. "The Mother of All Dogs." *Time*, 2 December 2002, 78-79.

Lloyd, Ann. *Hollywood Dogs*. New York: Barron's Educational Series, 2004.

Mahood, Jay. "A Few Good Dogs." *AKC Gazette*, June 2006, Vol. 123 No. 6, 34-37.

Niblock, Margaret. *The Afghan Hound: A Definitive Study*. New York: ARCO Publishing Inc., 1980.

O'Neill, Amanda. *Dogs*. New York: Kingfisher, 1999.

O'Neill, Thomas. "Traveling the Australian Dog Fence." *National Geographic*. April 1997:18-35.

Palmer, Joan. *Dog Facts*. New York: Barnes and Noble Books, 1991.

Parker, Heidi G., "Genetic Structure of the Purebred Domestic Dog." *Science*, 21 May 2004, 1160-1164.

Rice, Dan. *Akitas*. New York: Barron's Educational Series, 1997.

Rowley, Barbara. "Speed Kills." *All Animals*, Spring 2006, 18-19.

Scott, Desiree. *The Borzoi*. England: Kingdom Books, 1999.

Sikora Siino, Betsy. *Alaskan Malamutes*. New York: Barron's Educational Series, 1997.

Singer, Marilyn. *A Dog's Gotta Do What a Dog's Gotta Do: Dogs at Work*. New York: Henry Holt, 2000.

Soy, Teri. *Guide to Owning a Shih Tzu*. United States of America: T.F.H. Publications, 1996.
Thornton, Kim. *Why Do Dogs Do That? Real Answers to the Curious Things Dogs Do*. California: BowTie Press, 1997.
von der Leyen, Katharina. *Illustrated Guide to 140 Dog Breeds*. New York: Barron's Educational Series, 2000.
White, Jo Ann. *The Shih Tzu: An Owners Guide to a Happy Healthy Pet*. New York: Howell Book House,1995.
Wilcox, Bonnie. *The Atlas of Dog Breeds of the World*. USA: T.F.H. Publications, Inc.,

Websites
www.bbc.co.uk/wales/southwest/halloffame/public_life/thecorgi.shtml
www.acdca.org/standard.html
www.alaskanmalamute.org/malhist.htm
www.tsamc.org/tsamc/faq/faq.html
www.pbs.org/wgbh/nova/dogs/evolution.html
www.cattledog.com/life/kids.html
www.natural-dog.com/philo/breed/history.htm
findagrave.com/cgi-bin/fg.cgi?page=gr&GSmpid=46585747&GRid=8634412
bakerinstitute.vet.cornell.edu/public_info/king_buck.html
www.pembrokecorgi.org/introd.htm
www.naturalsciences.org/conservation/invasives/cat.html
rarebreed.com/breeds/orchid/orchid_hist.html
neapolitan.com/restore.htm
www.neapolitan.com/semen.html
www.brookmanstamps.com/netcat/federal/rw26info.html
bhlegends.com/breedhistory.html
www.pbs.org/lewisandclark/inside/seaman.html
www.pbs.org/wgbh/nova/dogs/
rarebreed.com/breeds/neo/neo_ukc_std.html
www.neapolitan.org/breed/breed.html